HOT SPOT!

by Virginia A. Arnold

illustrated by Benrei Huang

MACMILLAN/McGRAW-HILL SCHOOL PUBLISHING COMPANY
New York Chicago Columbus

Down by the bay
When it is hot,

My mother and I
Make rhymes a lot.

Hot spot! Hot spot!
Can you rhyme or can you not?

I can rhyme, but I forgot.
Help me make a rhyme for **spot**!

Spin! Spot!
I'm so hot!

Trip! Trot!
Now I'm not!

My mother and I
Make rhymes a lot!

Now will you rhyme,
Or will you not?